Write your name:

Qu qu

On sunny days, Inky, Snake, and Bee go to see the ducks.
Inky pretends her paws are a beak and shouts *qu*, *qu, qu*, *qu*.

Action: Make a duck's beak with your hands and open and close it, saying *qu, qu, qu, qu*.

In English words, ‹q› is always followed by ‹u›. The letters ‹q› and ‹u› make the sound /qu/ – not just ‹q›. The letter ‹q› borrows the sounds of ‹k› and ‹w›.

You never write ~~kw~~ always **qu** ✓

qu

qu qu qu qu qu

qu qu qu qu

___ack

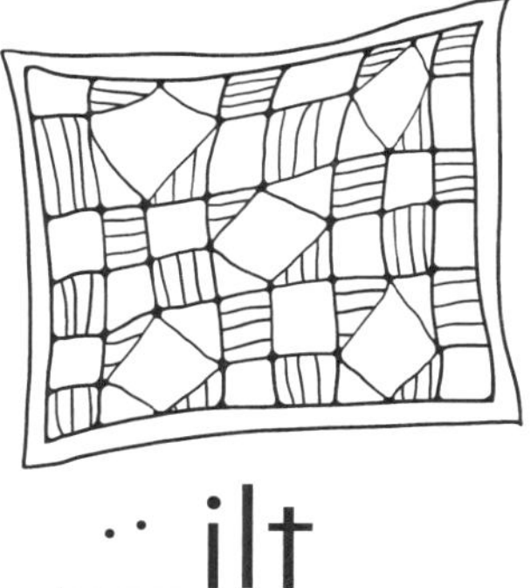

___ilt

quick quiz quit

"Ou!" cried the girl, "I've pricked my thumb with the needle."

ou

Action: Pretend your finger is a needle and prick your thumb, saying *ou!*

ouch ouch

ouch ouch

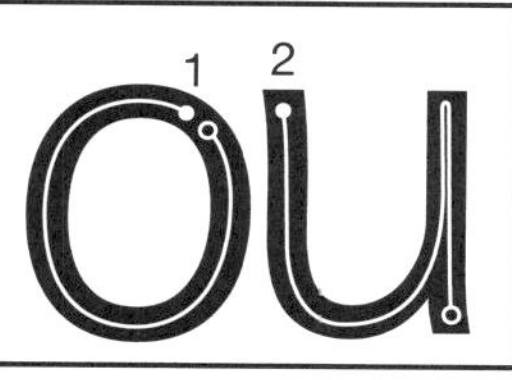

ou ou ou ou ou

ou ou ou ou

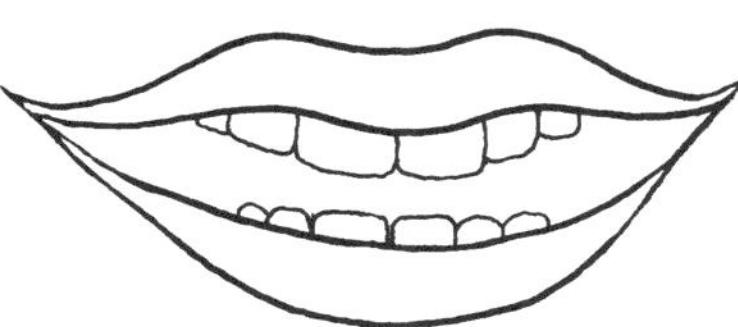

cl__d

h__se

m__th

count round shout

oi

"Oi, ship ahoy!" shouted the captain of the ship.

Action: Cup your hands around your mouth as if you are hailing a passing boat, and say *oi, ship ahoy!*

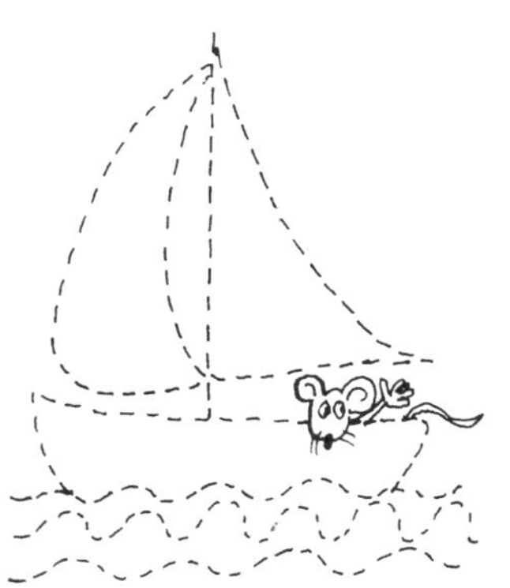

oi! oi! oi!

oi! oi! oi!

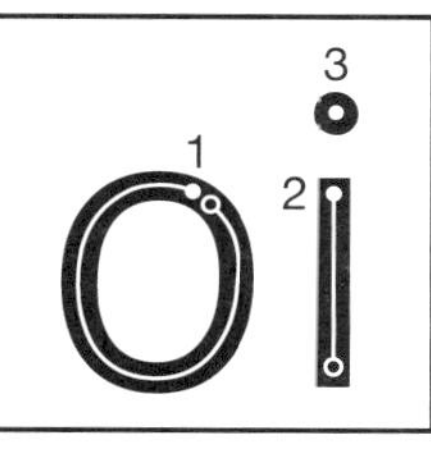

oi oi oi oi oi

oi oi oi oi oi oi

p__nt

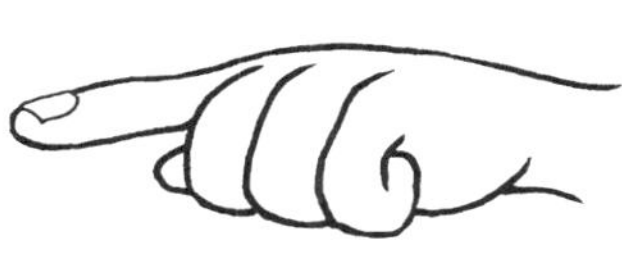

c__n

b__l

foil

joint

spoil

ue

Inky, Snake, and Bee are playing “Guess Who?” When the music stops they guess who has the ring, pointing and saying *ue*.

Action: Point to people around you, and say *ue, ue, ue, ue*.

ue ue ue

ue ue ue

ue

ue ue ue ue

ue ue ue ue ue ue

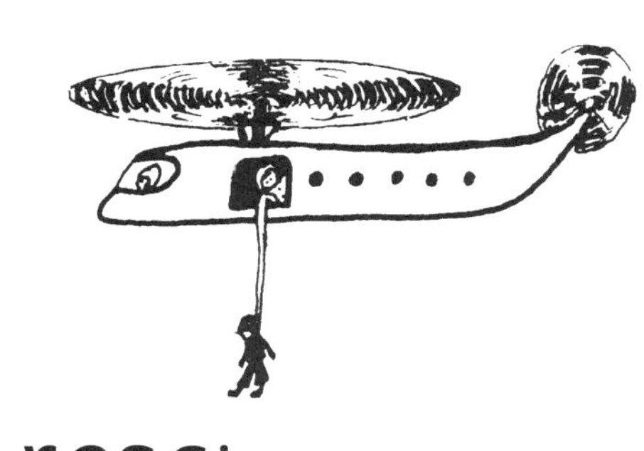

resc__

f__l

stat__

cue

continue

value

Inky is making some gingerbread people. She mixes up all the ingredients with a mixer: *er-er-er-er.*

Action: Roll your hands over each other like a mixer, and say *er-er-er-er.*

How to make your book

1. Pull out the middle section of your workbook (pages 11–14).
2. Cut along the centerfold. Place this page on top of the other.
3. Cut along the dotted line. Put the upper two sheets on top of the others.
4. Fold to make your book.
5. Check your page numbers. The title page should be at the front.

Note: This book is intended for use when the children have completed their workbooks, including the tricky words.

16

The Bad-Tempered Goat

1

Then he butts the tree trunk. Crick, crack, crunch!

12

He shouts and butts his horns against the tree trunk.

5

Farmer Green lives on Moat Farm.

2

The goat promises never to get bad-tempered again.

Farmer Green is feeding all his animals.

6

The goat starts to get cross. He stomps and kicks.

11

Farmer Green has to get out his tractor to help the goat get free.

14

He keeps different animals on his farm.

3

Then he swoops and sits on the goat's horns.

10

He has just given the goat his oats, when...

7

The goat has a bad temper.

4

He butts the tree again. Crack! It drops on him. He is stuck.

13

...a robin has a quick peck at the oats and hops up into the oak tree.

8

"Good morning," he shouts to the goat.

9

er er er mixer

er er er mixer

er er er er er er

er er er er er

lett__

butt__

dinn__

winter summer sister

ar

A big sea lion sits
at the top of some
rocks and barks,
ar, *ar*, *ar*!

Action: Clap your hands loosely like a seal, saying, *ar*, *ar*, *ar*, *ar*.

Trace the dotted line and reach the chart on the island. Watch out for the sharks!
ar
1
2
c
sc f
st
park
shark
jar

Caterpillar ‹c› is important because it is the starting point for many other letters. Practice these letters that start with caterpillar ‹c›.

c

a

d

o

g

q

In each of these words there is a letter that is not making its sound. These letters are written in faint type. You do not need to say the sound of a faint letter when blending. Read the words and draw a picture.

mouse	**lam**b	k**nee**
goose	**s**w**ord**	**hous**e
juggle	**appl**e	**puzzl**e

Write the lower-case letters next to their capitals.

Read the words and find them in the picture. Write some short phrases about something you can see in the picture.

net	rock	pool	boat	gull
float	sail	sand	swim	

a man with a hat

Tricky words: How quickly can you read them all?

to do are I was all

1 2 3 4 5 6 7

Count the rocks.

In this last book in the series, the numbers 8 and 9 are included. Trace over the dotted lines to write the numbers 7, 8, 9.

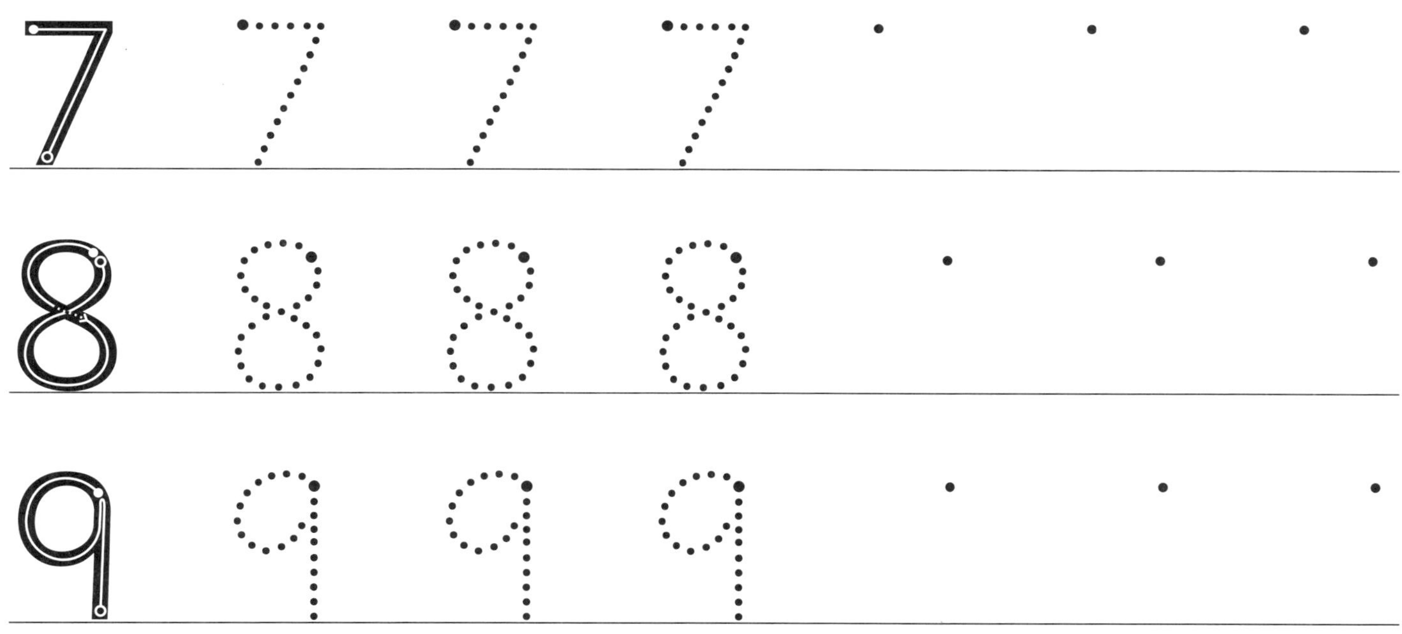

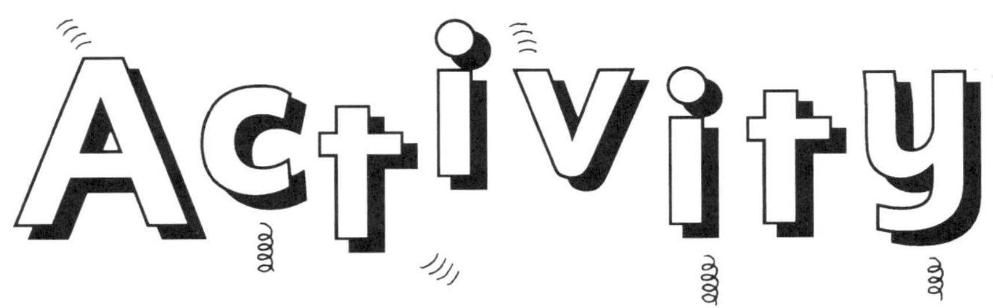

Add a *ue* tree to your vowel forest (from Workbook 4, p.24)

Make gingerbread people

Decorate them with currants or icing.

Make a star and clouds picture

Collect *ar* words to go in the stars and *ou* words for the clouds.

Ouch!

Read the story of Sleeping Beauty, who pricked her finger on a needle.